Last Post
BY CAROL ANN DUFF

In all my dreams, before my helpless sight,
He plunges at me, guttering, choking, drowning.

If poetry could tell it backwards, true, begin
that moment shrapnel scythed you to the stinking mud...
but you get up, amazed, watch bled bad blood
run upwards from the slime into its wounds;
see lines and lines of British boys rewind
back to their trenches, kiss the photographs from home –
mothers, sweethearts, sisters, younger brothers
not entering the story now
to die and die and die.
Dulce – No – Decorum – No – Pro patria mori.
You walk away.

You walk away; drop your gun (fixed bayonet)
like all your mates do too –
Harry, Tommy, Wilfred, Edward, Bert –
and light a cigarette.
There's coffee in the square,
warm French bread
and all those thousands dead
are shaking dried mud from their hair
and queuing up for home. Freshly alive,
a lad plays Tipperary to the crowd, released
from History; the glistening, healthy horses fit for heroes, kings.

You lean against a wall,
your several million lives still possible
and crammed with love, work, children, talent, English beer, good food.
You see the poet tuck away his pocket-book and smile.
If poetry could truly tell it backwards,
then it would.

Introduction to the fourth reprint
The row about the war

The last veteran of the trenches is dead. This is fortunate for our rulers. Were he still alive, Harry Patch's voice would be heard denouncing their jingoism and warmongering as we enter the centenary of the First World War.

Patch had lived in the filth of the trenches, 'gone over the top' at Passchendaele, and seen the bodies of men torn apart by flying metal. He had not wanted to go: he was conscripted. He had not wanted to kill: he made a pact with his mates never to kill a German. He hated all war until the day he died (in 2009). He told Tony Blair to his face that 'war is organised murder'.

Now that he is gone, the ground is clear for politicians like Michael Gove, broadcasters like Jeremy Paxman, and military historians like Max Hastings to 'revise' the history of the First World War.

Why does it matter so much? Why are they expending so much energy on rewriting history to make the war a Boy's Own tale of heroism, glory, and noble sacrifice, with wicked Huns on one side and upright Brits on the other?

The row about the First World War is an argument about our own world. The 'War on Terror' has now raged for almost a decade and a half. It has spread death and destruction across a huge swathe of North Africa, the Middle East, and Central Asia. It has generated escalating spirals of instability and violence, and our rulers have lost control over the regions they sought to dominate in the interests of profit and power. And they have faced rolling waves of mass anti-war protest at home on a scale never seen before.

Education Secretary Michael Gove was livid and abusive when the Tories lost the Commons vote over Syria on 30 August 2013. They had been prevented from starting another war, and Defence Secretary Philip Hammond was in no doubt about why: he was on Newsnight within half an hour saying that Iraq had 'poisoned the well of public opinion'.

For the first time since 1782 a British prime minister had been defeated on a war vote. The government's foreign policy had been shredded. Army chiefs were left fretting at growing constraints on the use of force. The limits of Western imperial power stood exposed.

This is the context for the row about the First World War. This is why Michael Gove kicked off the New Year by announcing that the British went to war in 1914 to defend 'the Western liberal order', that left-wing teachers and academics denigrate 'patriotism, honour, and courage', and that Britain's role in the world reflects its 'special tradition of liberty'.

Gove leads the government charge, but he is backed by David Cameron, Boris Johnson, and many other leading Tories.

Jeremy Paxman, meantime, is heading up the BBC's planned 2,500 hours of First World War coverage. 'German troops were on the march throughout Europe,' he tells us; they had 'detailed plans for the conquest of Europe'. The British helped roll back the tide, and this, apparently, 'forged the country we know today'.

Industrialised warfare thus becomes a form of moral redemption. 'I'd have done better for having time in uniform,' says Paxman. 'Obviously I'm not wishing war on anyone, but it might have been better for all of us if we'd been obliged to do something rather than choosing for ourselves.' So First World War revisionism becomes an explicit argument for conscription, national service, and imperialist war.

These arguments are backed by leading right-wing historians. Max Hastings argues that Austria and Germany were to blame for the war, that 'the war poets' view' of the conflict is false, and that 'it was vital to the freedom of Europe that the Kaiser's Germany should be defeated'.

This is only the beginning. The British government, along with many others, is engaged in a series of major ceremonies to mark successive anniversaries in the history of the war. The media schedules are chock-full of revisionist commentators. Some 400 commemorative stones are to be laid in honour of VC winners.

The soldiers of the First World War made no distinction between medal-winners and the rest: they stood together as comrades-in-arms. Nor do our war cemeteries and war memorials make such distinctions: all of the fallen are treated equally. But the government now plans to reconfigure the First World War as a necessary war, fought by 'heroes', for democracy and civilisation. Imperialism and industrialised carnage are to be rehabilitated.

This pamphlet answers the Tory arguments about the First World War. It reveals the profiteering, empire-building, and arms race that lay behind it. It shows it to have been a war in the interests of the rich and their system. It sees the war as men like Harry Patch saw it: as a world gone mad.

It views the conflict from below and finds that it was contested – before it started, while it raged, and, above all, as it ended. It discovers a hidden history of pacifism, anti-war activism, and militant trade-unionism. And it finds hope and inspiration in the growing tide of mutinies, strikes, demonstrations, and, finally, full-scale revolution that ended the killing and showed that another world was possible.

The First World War today

Tory Prime Minister David Cameron is spending £55 million on commemo-rating the centenary of the First World War. His aim is to celebrate 'Britishness' and what he calls 'our national spirit'.

Speaking at a press conference at the Imperial War Museum in October 2012, Cameron made the announcement in front of Paul Nash's painting *The Menin Road*.

The title is ironic. There is no road in the picture. It has been destroyed by shell-fire. Instead, stretching to the horizon is a landscape of mud, tree stumps, ruined buildings, barbed wire, water-filled craters, and the concrete blocks and corrugated iron of shattered bunkers. Shells explode in the distance. Four soldiers pick their way through the mire.

The Menin Road depicts the battlefield of Passchendaele in Flanders. It was, wrote war poet Wilfred Owen, 'a sad land, weak with sweats of death, grey, cratered like the moon with hollow woe, and pitted with great pocks and scabs of plagues'. For in this place, during three months of drenching rain in 1917, two million men fought each other for possession of patches of slime and rubble.

As the British Army's heavy guns, one for every five yards of front, fired millions of shells in a creeping barrage of high explosive, the attacking infantry stumbled forwards knee-deep in muck towards the German defences.

These were several miles deep, a spider's web of trenches, bunkers, and machine-guns nests laced with thickets of barbed-wire. Thousands were cut down by the storm of steel as they went in. Many of the wounded were sucked into the mud and disappeared forever. Those who got through were soon consumed in a primeval close-quarters struggle with firearms, bombs, and clubs inside a maze of shell-smashed trenches reeking of gas, shit, and rotting bodies.

'We came across a lad from A Company,' remembered Harry Patch, an old soldier who died in 2009, the last veteran of the trenches.

> *He was ripped open from his shoulder to his waist by shrapnel, and lying in a pool of blood. When we got to him, he looked at us and said, 'Shoot me'. He was beyond all human help, and before we could draw a revolver he was dead. And the final word he uttered was 'Mother'... I remember that lad in particular. It is an image that has haunted me all my life, seared into my mind ...*

When it ended, the Battle of Passchendaele had changed nothing. The opposing lines had moved a few miles, but were as strongly defended as ever. The stalemate was unbroken. The war went on.

The fallen

The cost of Passchendaele's nothing was more than half a million dead and wounded. Many of the dead were listed as 'missing'. Most are still there, their bodies preserved in the solidified mud of Flanders like prehistoric flies in resin. 'I was hobbling back,' wrote Siegfried Sassoon, another war poet, 'and then a shell burst slick upon the duckboards, so I fell into the bottomless mud, and lost the light.'

Tyne Cot cemetery contains the graves of 12,000 of the men who died in the mud of Passchendaele. Of these, 70% are unidentified. Bodies were hauled from the morass, but the mud had sucked away their identity. Others were never found at all. Inscribed on the back wall of the cemetery are the names of 35,000 'missing': names without bodies; names of men who had simply vanished from the face of the earth.

Passchendaele. Let it stand for hundreds of other industrialised battles fought on three continents during four years of world war. Other battles on the Western Front, like the Marne, Verdun, and the Somme. Battles on a similar scale on the Eastern Front, between Russians, Germans, and Austrians. Battles in the Alps, where half a million Italians perished in eleven separate assaults up the same blood-drenched slopes. Battles in Macedonia between Serbs, Bulgars, and Greeks; and battles on the Gallipoli Peninsula between Briton, Australian, and Turk. Battles in the snow of the Caucasus Mountains, where Turkish peasant-conscripts fought Russian peasant-conscripts, and battles in the deserts of Iraq, Jordan, and Palestine, where Turkish peasant-conscripts fought dockers from East London, sheep-hands from New Zealand, and farmers from Punjabi villages. And battles in Africa, where 100,000 black porters were worked to death in a white man's war.

The killing surpassed all precedent. No-one is quite sure how many died. Certainly 10 million. Possibly 20 million. And whatever the total, around twice as many again were wounded, often maimed or disfigured, and uncounted others driven insane. Tens of millions more were left grieving forever for a son, brother, husband, father, or lover who never returned.

What made it so long and deadly was that war had been turned into an industrial process.

Industrialised warfare

The First World War transformed modern society's capacity to satisfy human need through mass production into its opposite: industrialised slaughter.

Mass conscription created armies of millions. The Prussian army at Waterloo in 1815 had numbered 60,000. Its successor a century later, the German army on the Western Front in 1914, numbered 1.5 million.

Mass production provided the uniforms, equipment, guns, munitions, and supplies to sustain such armies. The British had had 156 guns at Waterloo in 1815, and these had fired a few thousands rounds in total during a day of battle. At the Somme in 1916 they had 1,600 guns. These fired nearly two million shells in the first few days. The battle lasted four and a half months.

Modern firepower created an impenetrable 'storm of steel' and an 'empty battlefield'. Men crawled from shell hole to shell hole, sheltered in the rubble of bombed-out buildings, or tunnelled into the ground. Stalemate and attrition shaped the entire conflict.

Industrial output was decisive: the demand was always for more guns, more shells, more explosive. Millions of workers were mobilised in war industries. Women left the home and fled domestic service to work in munitions factories. The home front became a target of bombing and blockade.

Once unleashed, the dynamic of industrialised militarism produced ever more lethal means of destruction. A technological arms race took off as rival scientists and engineers competed to increase their nations' killing power. In 1914 the British Army had no motorised trucks and only a few dozen reconnaissance aircraft. By 1918 they had 56,000 trucks and 22,000 aircraft. They also had new weapons: the trench mortar, the light machine-gun, and the tank.

War was no longer the business of small professional armies campaigning in distant places. It had become a monstrous mechanism of destruction that engulfed entire societies. Millions were conscripted. Millions worked in munitions factories or laboured on the land to feed the war-machine. Millions starved as consumption collapsed. Germany lost 1.8 million soldiers in the war, but almost half that number again died of hunger at home.

Bits of coloured cloth

Cheering crowds had greeted the outbreak of war. Millions had willingly answered the call to fight. They went because their lives were drab and they craved adventure; or because their mates were going and they did not want to be thought a 'coward'; or because they were sold what Wilfred Owen called 'the old lie': *dulce et decorum est pro patria mori* – 'it is sweet and glorious to die for one's country'.

Europeans marched into the maelstrom under a dozen different flags. All were told the same tale: their country was in danger and they were fighting to defend it. The enemy was demonised as an aggressive primitive. Medieval myths were reconfigured in the service of modern industrialised war.

Across the fighting fronts, at the behest of warlords and millionaires, peasants and workers on one side fought peasants and workers on the other. Britons fighting for 'King and Country' and Frenchmen for '*La Patrie*' killed Germans fighting for 'Kaiser and Fatherland'. Germans recast as medieval 'Teutons' killed Russians recast as medieval 'Slavs'. Italian against Austrian, Serb against Bulgar, Turk against Armenian – everywhere the same: dormant nationalism, charged with racism, was stirred into a violent storm of mass murder.

'Flags,' said Indian writer and anti-war activist Arundhati Roy, 'are bits of coloured cloth that governments use first to shrink-wrap people's minds and then as ceremonial shrouds to bury the dead.' So it was now.

Harry Patch thought the war 'a licence to go out and murder'.

Why should the British government call me up and take me out to a battlefield to shoot a man I never knew, whose language I couldn't speak? All those lives lost for a war finished over a table. Now what is the sense in that?

David Cameron, speaking before a painting of Passchendaele, argues otherwise. Unburdened by any sense of irony, he wants the centenary of the First World War to be a nationalist carnival, like the Diamond Jubilee and the London Olympics.

We must ensure that it is not. In active opposition to the stupidity and warmongering of politicians, we must make the centenary an act of international remembrance, understanding, and solidarity.

Their history and ours

The Somme was Britain's bloodiest battle. The 60,000 casualties suffered in three weeks of fighting at the Battle of Loos the previous autumn had been considered shocking enough. Now, as the Battle of the Somme began on 1 July 1916, the British Army suffered 60,000 casualties *in a single day*. The final total for the four-and-a-half month battle was almost half a million.

The Somme was the first big battle of the 'New Armies' of wartime volunteers. The old Regular and Territorial Armies had been consumed in the battles of 1914 and 1915. The men who fought on the Somme were among the hundreds of thousands who had joined up in the patriotic fervour of autumn 1914.

So the battle was a massacre of innocents, of enthusiastic but uninitiated citizen-soldiers. The unprecedented slaughter turned the mood in the trenches to one of sombre resignation. It plunged a score of working-class communities back home into mourning. It transformed middle-class patriots into anti-war poets, and created a mass audience for anti-war activists.

The Somme, along with Passchendaele, remain seared into the collective psyche of the British people, a cultural memory sustained by the poetry, memoirs, images, dramatisations, and museum displays that have stood testimony to the misery and horror of the trenches for almost a century.

The consensus is that the First World War was a colossal and pointless waste of human life; that it represented a world gone mad.

This is a source of growing frustration to many right-wing historians. Determined to rehabilitate ideas of empire, nationalism, and war, they have mounted increasingly effective attacks on the anti-war consensus. They now trumpet 'a revolution in the historiography of the First World War', and, from elevated perches inside the universities, profess disdain for what they regard as the simplistic prejudices of a popular audience that prefers to remain in ignorance.

These 'revisionist' arguments underlie the official commemorations. Let us review them.

The 'necessary sacrifice' theory

Revisionist perspectives do not ignore the mud and blood. But these are now accompanied by explanatory texts which speak of 'necessary sacrifice' in a war to defeat 'German militarism' and restore 'the balance of power'. The carnage on the Somme and at Passchendaele is hailed as a struggle between good and evil.

Revisionism boils down to three linked arguments. First, that long battles of attrition were necessary to wear down the German Army and pave the way to victory. Second, that this victory was necessary because Germany was an aggressive state that threatened world peace. And third, that Germany was a particularly predatory, militaristic, and ruthless imperial power.

These are very old arguments. They were used at the time by the leaders of Britain and France to justify the war, and afterwards to justify their own empire-building. This is the myth of German 'war guilt'. It is now being given a new lease of life.

Gary Sheffield argues that 'the behaviour of Germany and Austria-Hungary was the most important factor in bringing about the war'; that Germany pursued a 'bellicose and clumsy foreign policy'; and that Germany seized on the assassination at Sarajevo 'to achieve its grand strategic aims, even at the risk of bringing about a general war'.

German malevolence becomes the explanation of an entire geopolitical epoch. Both Britain and France

> *...were near-democracies...and neither relished the idea of the victory of autocratic Germany. Berlin, by contrast, planned to reduce France to a second-class power, to turn Belgium into a protectorate, and to create* Mitteleuropa, *a German-dominated economic zone in the centre of Europe. By the end of the war, Germany was busy carving an empire out of the ruins of defeated Russia. These expansionist plans had a good deal of continuity with those of the Third Reich.*

The 'good empires' theory

The implication is that the policies of 'near-democratic' France and Britain were measured and reasonable, while those of 'autocratic' Germany were not; and perhaps the further implication that this difference arose *because* the former were 'near-democracies' and Germany an 'autocracy'.

This attempt to discern clear differences – effectively moral differences – between the great powers has been popularised by TV historian Niall Ferguson. He elevates the British Empire into an historical model suitable for emulation – specifically by the contemporary American Empire.

The crudeness of Ferguson's widely trumpeted argument is alarming. While the Germans were exploiting and terrorising colonial populations, the British were supposedly promoting commerce, providing clean government, establishing the rule of law, and preparing their colonies for an eventual transition to parliamentary democracy.

Revisionist arguments like these supply the academic gloss to the banalities of politicians who want to use the centenary of the First World War to celebrate 'Britishness'.

This pamphlet stands in a different tradition. It aims to explain the real causes and consequences of the First World War.

How it started

On 28 June 1914, a Serbian nationalist student assassinated the heir to the Austro-Hungarian throne during a state visit to Sarajevo in Bosnia. Five weeks later, Austria, Russia, Germany, France, and Britain were at war. How did this happen?

The assassination at Sarajevo did not at first cause general alarm. Even in Austria-Hungary, the event seemed remote from everyday concerns in cities like Vienna and Budapest. Economic growth, a confident middle class, a boom in grand architecture, and a flourishing of science and the arts had turned the previous 20 years into what some called *la belle époque* – 'the beautiful age'.

The mood was different in the secret conclaves of the Austro-Hungarian state. Austria-Hungary was a ramshackle dynastic empire in the heart of Europe ruled by the German-speaking Habsburgs. Its 39 million people comprised: 12 million Austrians, 10 million Hungarians, 6.6 million Czechs, 5 million Poles, 4 million Ukrainians, 3.2 million Croats, 2.9 million Rumanians, 2 million Slovaks, 2 million Serbs, 1.3 million Slovenes, and 0.7 million Italians.

The Austrian and Hungarian ruling classes ran the empire in tandem. The ageing Habsburg autocrat Franz Josef was both Emperor of Austria and King of Hungary.

The Habsburg regime was threatened by the militancy of a growing working class and by mounting nationalist agitation among its subject-peoples. It responded with an unstable mix of repression and reform. By 1914 constitutional government had broken down and hawks like top general Conrad von Hötzendorf had taken control.

'Only an aggressive policy … can save this state from destruction,' he argued. The authority of the state was to be reasserted by demonstrative military action.

The target was Serbia, an independent Balkan state that acted as a beacon of resistance for Slavic people living under Austrian rule. Conrad had pressed for war against Serbia – 'this viper' – 25 times between 1906 and 1914. The assassination at Sarajevo was his golden opportunity.

On 23 July the Austrian government issued an ultimatum accusing the Serbs of complicity in the assassination and threatening war if they did not co-operate fully in its investigation and the suppression of anti-Austrian agitation on their territory.

Dissatisfied with the Serbian response, on 28 July the Austrians ordered mobilisation for war against Serbia and opened fire on Belgrade. These were the first shots of the First World War.

with the French and the Russians.

This had imposed an unsustainable military burden on Germany. The French and Russian armies had been growing at the same time as the British fleet. Germany was a continental power with enemies on two sides. It had therefore been forced to abandon the naval arms race and switch its main effort to army expansion. Germany could not both defend itself in Europe and challenge Britain at sea.

By late 1912 German leaders were convinced they were losing the European arms race and that the balance of forces was tipping against them. They came to favour a pre-emptive war sooner rather than later. The leader of the German Army, Helmuth von Moltke, argued that 'a war of nations' was unavoidable.

An imperialist war

The First World War was caused by military competition between opposing alliances of nation-states. These nation-states represented the interests of rival blocs of capital competing in world markets.

The British were able to adopt a holier-than-thou attitude because they had grabbed the biggest empire in the 18th century and then led the industrial revolution in the 19th. They favoured free trade because they were economically established.

They were able to portray the Germans as 'aggressors' and 'militarists', and to claim they were 'guilty' of starting the war, only because they were defending an existing empire rather than trying to create a new one.

But the underlying aims of the rulers of all the great powers were identical: to carve-up the world in pursuit of profit and power. The First World War was an imperialist war.

Could it have been stopped?

Such was the build-up of tension and military power before 1914, and such the rapid slide into war in the last few days as one mobilisation triggered another, that the First World War can seem inevitable.

It was not. Bankers, industrialists, and generals had an interest in war. The working people of Europe and those living under colonial rule in Africa and Asia did not. Nor were the war's victims simply brainwashed by jingoism and led willingly to the slaughter.

As the storm clouds darkened in the decade before war broke out, millions joined anti-war protests. Europe in 1914 was a doubly divided continent – divided into rival geopolitical blocs, and divided between pro-war elites and anti-war mass movements.

Habsburg Austria-Hungary

Vienna, Prague, and Budapest, the three great cities of Austria-Hungary, had become cauldrons of discontent. The oppressed peoples ruled by Austrian and Magyar overlords were in revolt against 'the prison-house of nations' that held them captive. Bohemian miners and Viennese workers fought pitched battles with police as they struggled to build trade unions. Parliamentary assemblies were paralysed as politicians fragmented on class and ethnic lines. The constitution was suspended and Austria's ageing dynastic autocrat ruled by emergency decree.

'Dictatorship and force are justified,' bellowed the Austrian foreign minister. 'Only an aggressive policy … can save this state from destruction,' thundered the Austrian army leader. The Austro-Hungarian elite, facing popular revolt and the breakup of the state, saw authoritarian rule and imperialist war as an antidote to internal crisis.

For a while they were right. When war was declared on Serbia on 28 July, the streets filled with flags, ribbons, and bands playing martial music, with columns of marching soldiers in blue-grey uniforms and crowds of patriots urging them on with shouts of 'Death to the Serbian dogs!'

Tsarist Russia

It was the same in Russia. Since April 1912 rolling waves of mass strike action had been sweeping across the industrial centres. The movement had reached a high-point in July 1914. Over a million workers struck in the first seven months of the year, and events had culminated in that final month of peace in a great general strike in the capital city. Russia was again, as in 1905, on the brink of revolution.

But when the Tsar appeared on the balcony of the Winter Palace to announce the declaration of war on 2 August, the waiting crowd erupted into a tremendous singing of the national anthem. The strikes of a few days before were forgotten. War, as so often before and after, had for the moment welded the nation into one.

To prove its patriotism, the mob later attacked the German Embassy and German offices and shops, murdering a caretaker in the process. Russia's corrupt, vicious, tottering ruling class had been uncertain how the people would respond to war. Now it had its answer. War had trumped revolution. Nationalism had suffocated socialism. Portraits of the Tsar had replaced the banners of revolt.

Imperial Germany

Two days later, the *Reichstag* (the German Parliament) voted unanimously for war credits – despite the fact that 110 of the deputies were members of the opposition Social-Democratic Party (SPD).

The German SPD was the model for socialists everywhere and its leaders were dominant in the Second International of socialist parties. The Second International was committed to all-out opposition to war. The November 1912 Basle conference had agreed that if war threatened, members should 'exert every effort in order to prevent the outbreak of war by the means they consider most effective', and that if it actually broke out, they should 'intervene in favour of its speedy termination' and use 'the economic and political crisis created by the war to arouse the people and thereby hasten the downfall of capitalist class rule'.

It had made no difference. The German socialists voted for war. Just days before, on 28 July, there had been 100,000 anti-war demonstrators on the streets of Berlin. Across Germany, during four days of mass protest in the final days of peace, there had been no fewer than 288 anti-war demonstrations involving up to three-quarters of a million people.

The mass anti-war movement had been building since 1911. The SPD stood at its head. On 4 August the party vote in the *Reichstag* killed the movement stone-dead and delivered the working people of Germany into the hands of the aristocratic officer caste and its army.

Republican France

A similar pattern, with national variations, was followed across the whole of Europe. Leading French anti-war socialist Jean Jaurès had called for general strikes against war in France and Germany. On 31 July he was murdered in a Paris café by a right-wing assassin, just as the French anti-war movement receded before a great tide of nationalist demands for the recovery of Alsace-Lorraine, the two border provinces lost in the Franco-Prussian War of 1870-1871.

French generals proclaimed 'the spirit of the offensive'. Victory would come from *élan* (vigour), from *cran* (guts), from the offensive *à l'outrance* (to the limit). Passivity – defending fortresses and trenches – would breed decadence and defeatism.

Accordingly, as the war began, lines of French conscripts in blue coats and red trousers charged forwards into machine-guns and modern artillery waving flags and blowing bugles. The French lost a quarter of their men in the first month.

Liberal Britain

Britain, too, was gripped by political crisis in the summer of 1914. The Suffragettes had elevated the struggle for women's emancipation into a militant mass movement. A bitterly contested Home Rule Bill had brought Ireland, Britain's oldest and closest colony, to the brink of civil war. And four years of national strikes by miners, dockers, and railwaymen had culminated in the forging of a Triple Alliance of immense industrial power.

But Britain's Liberal Government, voted into power on a heady promise of radical reform in 1906, had long since been taken over by belligerent imperialists. In London no less than in other European capitals that summer, a tiny minority of warmongers was able to submerge mass movements of resistance under a tide of jingo and militarism.

They could have been stopped. Tens of millions were actively opposed to them. Hundreds of millions stood to gain from peace. But the necessary clarity of purpose and strength of will were lacking. Not at the bottom, among ordinary activists; at the top, among their leaders.

Instead of trying to turn the mass anti-war movement into a wave of protests, strikes, and mutinies powerful enough to stop the war, the leaders of the European labour movement capitulated to the nationalism and militarism of their own ruling elites. The price was to be 15 million dead.

Were the generals to blame?

The stereotype of the British Army during the First World War is of 'lions led by donkeys'. War memoirs like Edmund Blunden's *Undertones of War* and Robert Graves' *Goodbye to All That* and more recent satires like *Oh! What a Lovely War* and *Blackadder Goes Forth* conjure a picture of ignorant and incompetent generals, many of them cavalrymen trained in colonial small-wars, repeatedly sending tens of thousands of men to their deaths by ordering hopeless attacks.

The British Army was certainly class-ridden. So were all First World War armies. The degree to which men of merit might rise from the ranks varied from army to army, but class was always dominant. Senior officers often had aristocratic backgrounds. Junior officers were usually recruited from the middle class. Workers and peasants formed the rank-and-file of all armies, and few had any chance of ever becoming officers.

Because the war was about profit and power – because its purpose was to re-divide the world in the interests of one national-capitalist bloc as against another – there could be no democracy. Soldiers could not be allowed to debate why they were fighting, to elect their own officers, or to discuss strategy and tactics. The danger was that they might decide not to fight at all.

Instead, armies were held together by strict top-down discipline. Soldiers were often forced 'to go over the top' at gunpoint, and hundreds were shot for 'cowardice' – that is, because they were frightened.

Class division

The social gulf between officers and men meant stupidity and slaughter. Generals did not trust their own soldiers. Soldiers were not allowed to think for themselves. As attrition replaced the experienced soldiers of 1914 with wartime volunteers and conscripts, the distrust deepened.

'Neither our new formations nor the old divisions,' complained General Rawlinson, 'have the same discipline that obtained in our army a year ago.' So on the first day of the Somme (1 July 1916) his men were ordered to 'push forward at a steady pace in successive lines'.

Here was the ultimate insanity: men walking upright across no-man's-land in the face of fire from modern artillery, machine-guns, and magazine-rifles. The generals considered their citizen-soldiers only half trained and prone to panic, and, ensconced in comfortable mansions far from the front-line, they were removed from the realities of the modern battlefield.

Some of the famous 'Pals Battalions' – formed of workers who had joined up together from the same factories and neighbourhoods – lost three-quarters of their men within ten minutes of going over the top.

Class division is a poison that infects human organisation with bullying, stupidity, and waste. This is never more true than in war. The most effective armies in history have been those which have maximised democracy and empowered the rank and file.

But it was not an excess of upper-class incompetence that produced the stalemate and attrition of the trenches. It was inherent in industrialised warfare.

Weapon systems

The trenches have become symbolic of the slaughter. But they did not cause it. In fact, they provided protection from the 'storm of steel' on battlefields dominated by firepower. The rate of killing was higher during the 'war of movement' in the autumn of 1914 and again in the last year of the war.

The real reason for high casualties was the modern industry behind each of the great powers. This meant mass production capable of arming, equipping, and supplying armies of millions. It meant weapons far more technically advanced than ever before. This combination of mass and technology meant battlefields deluged with firepower.

The fighting fronts went into lock-down. The opposing trench systems were many miles deep, comprising three separate lines, one behind the other, each formed of three trenches, a front-line trench, a support trench, and a reserve trench. These were reinforced with concrete bunkers and protected by dense thickets of barbed wire. All approaches were covered by artillery and machine-guns. Trench battles were therefore long and murderous.

But battles in open ground were even more deadly. It was the killing-power of weaponry that was decisive, not tactics.

That is one reason the Second World War was longer and bloodier than the First. It lasted six years and killed 60 million compared with four years and 15 million. Stalingrad, for example, was a bloodier battle than any in the First World War. Global industrial capacity was that much greater 20 years later. It is highly likely that a world war today would be the worst in history.

The real criticism of men like Douglas Haig, the British commander-in-chief on the Western Front, is not that he was a 'donkey'. It is that he was a leading member of a rapacious ruling class prepared to sacrifice millions of ordinary men in a war for empire and profit.

The real indictment of battles like the Somme and Passchendaele is not that they were misconceived and mismanaged – though they unquestionably were – but that they were ever fought at all.

Total war

The German plan to defeat France in the first six weeks of the war failed. Though 1.5 million strong, the German army was not large enough to encircle Paris, the invasion lost momentum and cohesion, and an Anglo-French counterattack at the Battle of the Marne forced it back onto the defensive (August/ September 1914).

The two sides then engaged in a series of leapfrogging attempts to out-flank the other to the north. Each effort failed, producing 'a race to the sea' that extended the trench lines until they stretched all the way from Switzerland to The Channel (October/November 1914).

The 'war of movement' was over. Trench stalemate had begun.

Deadlock

The Germans remained on the defensive on the Western Front for most of the next four years. They occupied most of Belgium and much of north-eastern France. They could bargain from a position of strength. Their enemies were obliged to try and dislodge them.

Two factors made their line unbreakable. One was technological. Firepower had made massive advances, but military mobility and communications had not. Attacking infantry were simply consumed in a maze of trenches and bunkers many miles deep. Their own artillery could not get forward easily. There were no fast-moving armoured vehicles. Airpower was underdeveloped. Telephone lines were cut by shelling and commanders lost contact with their men. The battlefield became hopelessly 'sticky'.

This, though, depended on the second factor: the density of German soldiers and guns on the front. The German Army was able to form an un-breakable line because it was sustained by a large, skilled, hard-working population and the most productive factories in Europe.

The Eastern Front became deadlocked for a different reason. Here the ratio of men and guns to space was lower. Fronts were more weakly de-fended and breakthroughs were often possible. But poor communications over vast distances slowed down victorious armies and allowed defeated ones to fall back and build new trenches lines closer to their supply bases. The war became a see-saw of advance and retreat. Because of this, deci-sive victory was as elusive in the east as in the west, and the war every bit as bloody.

The entry of new belligerents – Ottoman Turkey, Bulgaria, and Italy – did not end the deadlock. It merely created new lines of trenches – in the Caucasus Mountains (today's Armenia), on the Gallipoli Peninsula (in European Turkey), in Mesopotamia (today's Iraq), in the southern Alps (from Switzerland to the northern Adriatic), and across the southern Balkans (from the southern Adriatic to the northern Aegean).

The war took on the form of a gigantic siege of the Central Powers (Germany, Austria-Hungary, Turkey, and Bulgaria) by the Entente Powers (Britain, France, Russia, Italy, Serbia, and, eventually, Greece and Rumania).

On the high seas, meantime, the British were blockading the German sea-lanes and waging a cat-and-mouse war against German cruisers and submarines. In the skies over Britain, German airships were opening a new chapter in the history of war by bombing cities hundreds of miles behind the front-lines. And in distant colonies, white officers were conscripting native peasants into labour-gangs to wage a gruelling bush war for control of Africa.

Attrition

The war of movement in 1914 gave way to a war of trenches in 1915. Attempts to break the stalemate by launching head-on attacks across no-man's-land were bloodily repulsed. Politicians and generals concluded they needed more men, more guns, more shells.

During the third phase of the war, in 1916 and 1917, hundreds of thousands of men and thousands of guns were mobilised in offensives sustained for months at a time. Verdun, the Somme, and Passchendaele were conceived as 'battles of attrition' designed to wear down the enemy by relentless industrial-scale killing.

'Within our reach behind the French sector of the Western Front,' announced General Falkenhayn, 'there are objectives for the retention of which the French General Staff would be compelled to throw in every man they have. If they do so, the forces of France will bleed to death ... whether we reach our goal or not.'

He was explaining his planned 1916 Verdun offensive. It lasted 10 months. The total cost was 700,000 men.

Attrition on this scale was made possible by 'total war' economies in which everything was sacrificed to the production of military *matériel*.

The war became an all-consuming monster of destruction. Economies were strained to breaking-point to fuel the fighting. Blockades further disrupted the flow of food and other essentials. Consumer prices soared. Consumption levels fell. Hunger stalked large swathes of Europe.

Such were the upheavals, and such the wretched condition of so many of the world's people, that disease ran rampant as the war neared its end. The

A peace to end all peace

They called it 'the war to end all war'. In fact, the victorious powers imposed 'a peace to end all peace', laying the foundations of another, longer, yet bloodier world war 20 years later.

The great revolutionary movement that convulsed Europe between 1917 and 1923 held out the promise of a world transformed – of mass democracy, of an economy geared to need not profit, of a new epoch of global peace.

It was not to be. Though shaken to its foundations, the old order of nation-states and giant corporations survived. The victors in a war of empire then set about re-dividing the world in their own interests.

The Versailles Treaty negotiated in the first half of 1919 stripped Germany of much of its territory in Europe and all of its overseas colonies, reduced its army to a token force, imposed crippling war reparations, and accused it of sole responsibility for the war.

Versailles was a gift to German nationalists. The indignation it engendered would fuel the rise of the Nazi Party and Hitler's programme of rearmament, revenge, and recovery.

The rulers of Britain and France were equally rapacious overseas. The fate of the peoples of Africa and Asia bears testimony to the lie that Britain and France had fought for democracy and that theirs were somehow 'good empires' and beacons of 'civilisation' and 'progress'.

Re-dividing the world

The French grabbed Togo and Cameroun in West Africa, and the British Namibia in Southern Africa and Tanzania in East Africa.

Far more Africans had died in the fighting in these countries than Europeans. Often this was because they had been conscripted as porters and then been beaten, starved, and worked to death. They now discovered what the war meant: the policemen had different uniforms. Exploitation by white farmers and mine bosses continued as before across the continent.

The British had promised the Arabs their independence, and the Arabs had fought alongside them to defeat the Ottoman Empire. But they had made a secret agreement with the French and the Russians to divide up the Ottoman Empire among themselves.

The imperial appetite was large: as well as the Arabic-speaking territories of the Middle East, the British and the French, along with their Italian and Greek allies, planned to take over Turkish-speaking Anatolia. The Turks were strong enough to prevent a carve-up of their national territory.

The Arabs were not – the French grabbed Syria and Lebanon, the British, Palestine, Jordan, and Iraq.

The British already controlled Egypt, and here their continuing presence provoked a major revolt in 1919 when they deported the leader of the nationalist Wafd party. Students marched through Cairo and rioting broke out across the city. This triggered further protests in the countryside. When the police opened fire and killed protestors, the funerals turned into huge nationalist demonstrations.

India, with its 250 million people, had been forced to contribute revenue, manpower, and supplies to feed Britain's war effort in Europe and the Middle East. Many Indians did not see why they should be fleeced for a white man's war on the other side of the world. When the war ended, demonstrations, strikes, and food riots swept the country.

Crushing revolt

On 16 April 1919 General Dyer ordered 50 riflemen to open fire on a demonstration inside a walled enclosure at Amritsar. They continued firing for ten minutes and killed up to 1,000 people.

As news of the massacre spread, resistance rose to new heights. Millions of peasants, workers, and urban poor become involved in mass action. Hindus and Muslims fought side by side against bosses, landlords, and police. The imperialist policy of divide and rule broke down as Indians of all backgrounds united against their foreign oppressors and the local rich. One British regional governor later admitted that the movement 'gave us a scare' and 'came within an inch of succeeding'.

Germany, like other European powers, had had colonies in China. These were handed over to the Japanese. Because of this, Chinese delegates refused to sign the Versailles Treaty, and when the news reached Beijing it detonated a new revolutionary movement. Student-led protests against imperialism unleashed a wave of action involving millions of ordinary Chinese, with mass meetings, demonstrations, boycotts of Japanese goods, and a general strike in Shanghai.

Meantime, on the other side of the world, the Irish were also in revolt against imperialism. The British had shelved Home Rule in 1914 and then crushed a premature nationalist revolt in 1916. But the subsequent execution of captured leaders outraged Irish opinion and gave Sinn Fein, the main nationalist party, a landslide victory in the general election of late 1918.

The Sinn Feiners refused to take their seats in the London Parliament and instead formed an independent Irish *Dáil*. The British waged a brutal colonial war against the Irish between 1919 and 1921. They failed to suppress the resistance and were forced to grant independence to Southern Ireland (though they succeeded in splitting the nationalists and securing the permanent partition of the island).

The behaviour of the victorious powers reveals the true character of the First World War: it was an imperialist war to re-divide the world. Its 15 million victims were precisely that: victims whose lives were wasted in a war for empire, profit, and the enrichment of a tiny minority of bankers and industrialists. The lives of the great majority, at home and in the colonies, continued to be blighted by poverty, violence, and police rule.

A century of war (and counting)

The century since the First World War began has been the bloodiest in human history. Humanity has counted the dead in tens of millions.

Gabriel Kolko, the radical historian of modern warfare, has called the 20th century 'the century of war'. The First World War did not 'end war'. It led to the Second World War, then the Cold War, and now the 'War on Terror' – an endless succession of wars powered by the competition of nation-states and giant corporations. Wars to decide which of the world's rich will get richer.

Because vast resources are devoted to weapons technology and the mass production of military hardware, killing-power is ever-increasing. Fifteen million died in the First World War, 60 million in the Second. Hundreds of millions would surely die if there was ever a Third.

On more than one occasion, tiny coteries of nuclear-powered pharaohs have huddled in underground bunkers and threatened humanity with 'mutually assured destruction' – the Cuban Missile Crisis of 1962 the most memorable.

The possibility remains: should the masters of the universe so decide, thousands of intercontinental nuclear missiles could be activated and launched from silos, ships, and submarines in a matter of minutes.

When the first atomic bomb was dropped on Hiroshima in 1945, it exploded with the power 12,500 tons of TNT, created ground-level temperatures of 4,000°C, destroyed 90% of the city's buildings, and killed 45,000 people instantly and 45,000 more in slow agony in the days afterwards. Within 20 years, the great powers had amassed nuclear arsenals with around a million times the destructive power of the Hiroshima bomb.

Nuclear-armed superpower war has not happened yet. But a succession of regional wars backed by rival imperial powers has run unbroken since 1945. The French fought a long war against the Vietnamese at a cost of half a million lives, and then another long war against the Algerians at a cost of a million lives. The Americans resumed the struggle against the Vietnamese and the death-toll between 1960 and 1975 is estimated to have reached five million.

'War on Terror' rhetoric has replaced Cold War propaganda as the justification for present-day wars. But the aim is the same – the use of military power to underpin corporate wealth – and so is the result: hundreds of thousands killed and maimed, millions more displaced and impoverished.

Estimates for the death-toll in the Iraq War start at 100,000 and rise to a million. The devastation of the country has left much of the population in poverty and squalor.

Trillions of dollars are wasted on armaments every year, and the killing-power of modern military arsenals rises exponentially. The tonnage of munitions expended in war by the US per man-year of combat rose from one ton in the Second World War, to eight tons in the Korean War (early 1950s), to 26 tons at the height of the Vietnam War (1966-1971). The US dropped more munitions on Iraq during its six-week aerial bombing campaign in early 1991 than were dropped on Germany during the whole of the Second World War.

According to Gabriel Kolko, we have reached

a point in human development when the nature and quantity of weaponry makes war so dangerous and destructive that surviving another century without terrible nuclear or chemical-biological catastrophes remains the single greatest challenge confronting people everywhere.

Since 1914 our rulers have waged one murderous war after another in their pursuit of profit and power. David Cameron is one of them. He represents austerity at home and imperialism abroad. He wants the centenary of the First World War to be a celebration of 'Britishness'. He waves bits of coloured cloth over a world of poverty, violence, and injustice.

The real lesson of the First World War is that imperialism, militarism, and nationalism are the mass killers of an insane world. We must trumpet this message as part of the fight for a better future – for a world of peace, justice, and solidarity.